VIKINGS

HOWARD LINSKEY

SHROPSHIRE COUNTY SCHOOLS LIBRARY SERVICE	
12370	
PETERS	941.01
Dec-2014	£5.99

WOW! facts

Badger Publishing Limited
Oldmedow Road,
Hardwick Industrial Estate,
King's Lynn PE30 4JJ
Telephone: 01438 791037

www.badgerlearning.co.uk

2 4 6 8 10 9 7 5 3 1

Vikings ISBN 978-1-78464-034-7

Text © Howard Linskey 2014

Complete work © Badger Publishing Limited 2014

All rights reserved. No part of this publication may be reproduced, stored in any form or by any means mechanical, electronic, recording or otherwise without the prior permission of the publisher.

The right of Howard Linskey to be identified as author of this work has been asserted by him in accordance with the Copyright, Designs and Patents Act 1988.

Publisher: Susan Ross
Senior Editor: Danny Pearson
Publishing Assistant: Claire Morgan
Designer: Fiona Grant
Series Consultant: Dee Reid

Photos: Cover image: National Geographic/Getty Images
Page 5: © Troy GB images/Alamy
Page 6: © appleuzr/iStock
Page 7: © ClassicStock/Alamy
Page 8: © The Print Collector/Alamy
Page 9: c.Everett Collection/REX
Page 10: © Robert Harding Picture Library Ltd/Alamy
Page 11: © AlgolOnline/Alamy
Page 12: © National Geographic Image Collection/Alamy
Page 13: © National Geographic Image Collection/Alamy
Page 14: Steve Black/REX
Page 15: © Troy GB images/Alamy
Page 16: Andrzel Szkocki/REX
Page 17: © Dario Lo Presti/Alamy
Page 18: © North Wind Picture Archives/Alamy
Page 19: © Mary Evans Picture Library/Alamy
Page 21: © David Gowans/Alamy
Page 23: © Heritage Image Partnership Ltd/Alamy
Page 24: © bildbroker.de/Alamy
Page 26: © Ivy Close Images/Alamy
Page 27: © Ivy Close Images/Alamy
Page 28: © Tony Wright/earthscapes/Alamy
Page 29: © Ivy Close Images/Alamy
Page 30: © Mary Evans Picture Library/Alamy

Attempts to contact all copyright holders have been made.
If any omitted would care to contact Badger Learning, we will be happy to make appropriate arrangements.

VIKINGS

Contents

1. The Vikings — 5
2. Pirates — 8
3. Into battle — 14
4. Traders and settlers — 20
5. At home — 24
6. Viking Gods and Valhalla — 26
7. The end of the Vikings — 30

Questions — 31

Index — 32

Badger
LEARNING

Vocabulary

Anglo-Saxons
beserker
Danegeld
jewellery

longship
monastery
shield
Valhalla

1. The Vikings

Vikings were warriors who attacked other countries.

They were said to be brutal and cruel but they were also settlers and traders who made goods to trade and sell.

The Vikings ruled much of England and Scotland between 793 and 1066.

Viking countries

Vikings came from Denmark, Norway and Sweden.

They sailed across the sea to countries like England and Scotland. They even sailed as far as America, Russia and North Africa.

Vikings were not full-time soldiers. In the summer many Viking men would obey their chieftain and go on raiding parties, attacking buildings and stealing treasure.

But in the winter they were farmers and fishermen.

WOW! facts

It was the law that Vikings must own weapons. They had to carry them all the time.

2. Pirates

The Vikings were pirates, but instead of just attacking ships, they raided other countries looking for treasure, crops or farm animals to steal.

When the sea was rough it would take days to cross from Viking lands to England and Scotland.

They sailed in longships, which were flat-bottomed boats, so when the Vikings had crossed the sea they could sail up shallow rivers to attack monasteries and villages.

WOW! facts

Viking longships were also called 'Dragon Boats'.

Raiding

The first raid on England happened in the year 787 when three longships landed on the south coast in Dorset.

In the year 793, Vikings attacked the Christian monastery at Lindisfarne in the northeast of England.

Lindisfarne is also called 'Holy Island'. The monks there did not have weapons because they thought that God would keep their treasure safe.

Vikings were pagans who believed in different gods, so they did not care about upsetting a Christian god.

They burned the monastery, stole gold and silver, and took crops and cattle from the fields. They killed the monks or took them as slaves.

WOW! facts

The word 'Viking' means 'Pirate Raid'.

Slaves

As well as stealing crops and treasure, Vikings also took people back on their longships.

When they arrived home they made these people slaves.

Some of the slaves were made to do the jobs Vikings did not want to do.

Jobs done by slaves:
- spreading muck on the fields
- digging peat
- building walls

Other slaves were sold or traded for goods.

When slaves had children, their children became slaves too. Some people spent all their lives as slaves but some were given their freedom.

WOW! facts

The Viking word for slaves is 'thralls'.

3. Into Battle

Most Vikings went into battle with a long sword. However, some Vikings could not afford a sword, as they were very expensive, so they would use an axe instead.

Vikings would also carry a knife and use a small, round, wooden shield to protect themselves.

Vikings wore helmets on their heads made of leather or iron.

People used to think that all Viking helmets had horns or wings but it turns out that isn't true.

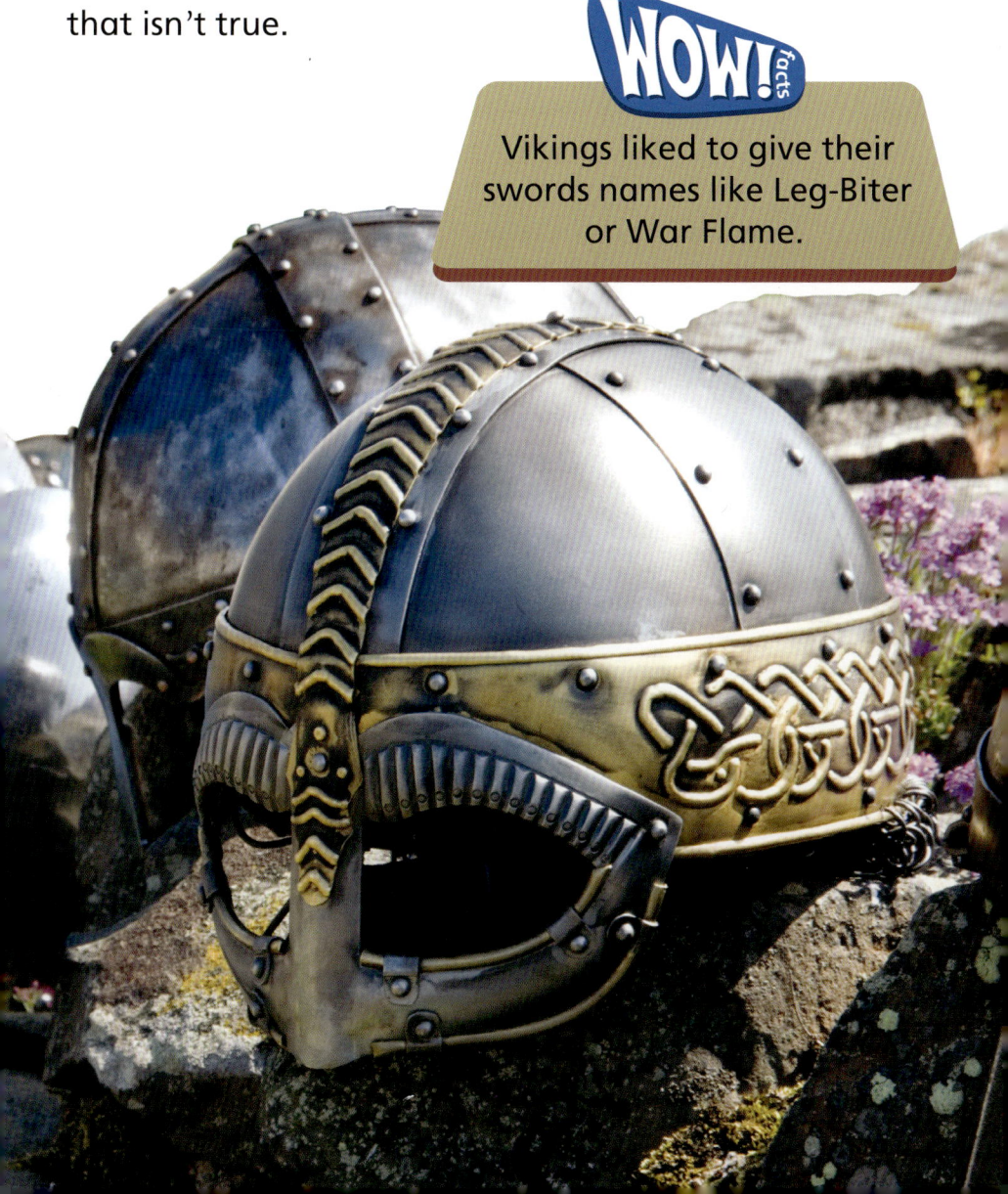

WOW! facts

Vikings liked to give their swords names like Leg-Biter or War Flame.

When Vikings went into battle they would line up young warriors in the front row, holding their shields to protect themselves. This was called a shield wall.

The older, better Viking fighters would stand behind the shield wall and throw spears or shoot arrows at the enemy.

The battles were fought with swords, axes and spears.

Twenty of the best warriors would charge the enemy shield wall to try to break through and win the battle by killing their enemy's leader.

This move was called the 'Boar's Snout'.

Berserkers

All Vikings were fierce warriors but the scariest were the berserkers. They went into battle without armour, dressed only in the skins of wolves or bears.

They worked themselves into a rage by getting drunk or taking drugs made from herbs or mushrooms. Then they fought wildly, lashing out at anyone who came near them.

Their enemies must have been terrified to see a man with no armour fighting so wildly.

The beserkers were so violent many Viking chieftains used them as bodyguards.

Hereward the Beserker in only a silk shirt, surrounded by men in armour.

WOW! facts

The word 'berserk' comes from berserkers. It means 'out of control with anger or excitement'.

4. Traders and settlers

When Vikings sailed to another country they did not always fight. Sometimes they traded goods instead.

What did Vikings sell or trade?
- honey
- wheat
- wool
- leather
- animal furs

What did Vikings buy?
- spices
- wine
- jewellery
- pottery

They bought these goods with gold and silver coins.

The people who lived in England were called Anglo-Saxons.

They called the Viking settlers 'Danes'. Over the years, many Vikings settled in England. The land they lived in became known as the Danelaw because Viking laws had to be obeyed there.

Danegeld

The Vikings were so powerful that after a while the Anglo-Saxons gave up trying to drive them out and decided to give them money instead.

The money they gave was called Danegeld and it was a tax the Anglo-Saxon king made his people pay.

He gave it to the Vikings to stop them from taking over his whole kingdom.

King Cnut

The Danish Prince Cnut sailed to England in 1015 with an army of 10,000 Vikings in 200 ships.

He fought the English for more than a year and beat Edmund, the English King.

He became a Viking King of England and ruled for 19 years.

WOW! facts

King Cnut was annoyed by flatterers always telling him he was master of land and sea – he was not so silly. So, one day, he sat on the sea-shore in his royal chair until the waves reached him, to prove that even kings cannot control the waves.

5. At Home

Women

Viking women did not fight with the men but stayed at home to look after the children.

They baked bread, made cheese and cooked meals for the family. They made clothes from the skins of animals or wool from sheep.

Women wore long wool or linen dresses, aprons and cloaks for warmth. They fastened their clothes with brooches and also wore bracelets or rings made of gold or silver.

Children

Viking children did not go to school and had no books to read.

They learned Viking history and law from stories told by their elders.

Boys were taught to fight from a young age so they could grow up to become warriors.

WOW! facts
Viking children had toys. They played with dolls or model ships carved from wood.

6. Viking Gods and Valhalla

Gods

Vikings did not believe in just one god. They believed there were many gods and each god was in charge of something.

Odin: chief of the Viking gods

Thor: Odin's son and god of thunder

Frigg: Odin's wife who could see into the future

Odin and Frigg

Odin was also called 'The One-Eyed' because he gave away one eye in exchange for the gift of wisdom.

Thor carried a hammer and Vikings believed that when Thor waved his hammer, lightning flashed across the sky.

Some days of the week are named after Viking gods. Thursday is named after Thor and Friday is named after Frigg.

Thor

Death and burial

Vikings believed that when they died they would still need their belongings.

They were buried with swords, tools and other useful items.

Sometimes their slaves were killed so they could serve their master in the next life.

Vikings believed in a heaven called Valhalla. This was a huge hall in a place called Asgard, ruled by the god Odin.

Vikings believed that warriors who died in battle went to Valhalla.

When someone died in battle, a Viking ship would be dragged onto land and the dead man placed inside.

The ship was then covered in soil for burial or burned.

7. The End of the Vikings

The Viking age in England came to an end when they were defeated at the Battle of Stamford Bridge by the Anglo-Saxon King Harold in 1066.

In that same year, William the Conqueror invaded England and he forced the Vikings to be ruled by him.

After that there were no more Viking kings in England.

Questions

Where did the Vikings come from? *(page 6)*

Why were longships flat-bottomed? *(page 9)*

What does the word 'Viking' mean? *(page 11)*

What were Viking helmets made of? *(page 15)*

For how long did King Cnut rule England? *(page 22)*

Why was the god Odin called 'The One-Eyed'? *(page 27)*

INDEX

Anglo-Saxons 21, 22, 30
armour 18, 19
axe(s) 14, 17
Battle of Stamford Bridge 30
berserkers 18-19
Danegeld 22
Danelaw 21
Denmark 6
Frigg 26-27
helmets 15
King Harold 30
Lindisfarne 10
longships 9, 10, 12
Norway 6
Odin 26-27, 29
Pagans 11
Prince/King Cnut 22-23
raiding parties 7
settlers 5, 21
shield 14, 16, 17
slaves 11, 12-13, 28
spears 16, 17
Sweden 6
sword(s) 14, 15, 17, 28
Thor 26-27
traders 5
treasure 8, 10, 12
Valhalla 29
William the Conqueror 30